The National Gallery
of Ireland *Concise Guide*

The National Gallery of Ireland *Concise Guide*

PUBLISHED BY THE NATIONAL GALLERY
OF IRELAND, 2002

FRONT COVER: The Baroque Room (Room 44)

BACK COVER: **Anton Raphaël Mengs** (1728-1779)
Thomas Conolly (1738-1803), Grand Tourist, 1758
Oil on canvas, 135 x 98 cm

TITLE PAGE: **Gerrit van Honthorst** (1590-1656)
A Concert Party, c.1616-18
Oil on canvas, 135.5 x 182 cm

©The National Gallery of Ireland 2002
First published 1996. Revised edition 2002
ISBN 0903162954

Original text by Alison Fitzgerald
Edited and Revised by Adrian Le Harivel
Design by Jason Ellams
Photography by Roy Hewson
Floorplan by Henrion, Ludlow & Schmidt
Typeset in Sabon
Printed in Belgium by Snoeck-Ducaju & Zoon, Ghent

Foreword

The National Gallery of Ireland houses
an exceptional treasury of visual art beautifully
presented in its rooms. It is a privilege for IIB
Bank to continue its long association with the
Gallery and to sponsor the publication of this
Concise Guide.

I hope that all visitors will find the Guide an
enhancement to their visit and an encouragement
to return many times.

The Short Guide is intended to give a sense of
the breadth of our collection and its highlights,
while placing them in the context of the Gallery's
history and development.

Through acquisition and many generous gifts
a truly representative collection of European art
has been formed, which is a source of delight and
instruction to visitors and frequently requested
for loan to exhibitions.

Entry to the Gallery is free and the welcome
support of IIB will enable this sample of its
riches to be equally accessible.

Edward A Marah
Chief Executive
IIB Bank

Raymond Keaveney
Director
National Gallery of Ireland

Introduction

1   **Stephen Catterson Smith
    the Elder** (1806-1872),
    William Dargan,
    (1799-1867), 1862.
    Oil on canvas, 72 x 57 cm

2   **James Mahoney** (1810-1879),
    *The Visit by Queen Victoria and Prince
    Albert to the Fine Art Hall of the
    Irish Industrial Exhibition*, c.1853.
    Watercolour on paper, 62.8 x 81 cm

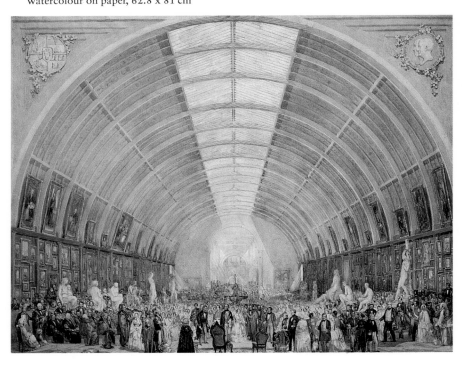

The earliest attempts to establish a public art
collection in Ireland date to the late eighteenth
century. In 1766 the Society of Artists considered
incorporating a gallery within their premises on
William Street in Dublin. Soon afterwards the
Duke of Rutland, Lord Lieutenant from 1784
to 1787, addressed the need for a national art
collection and appointed the artist Pieter de Gree
as Keeper of the proposed gallery. However,
with the Duke's untimely death, plans for the
gallery were shelved and it was not until the
mid-19th century that they reached fruition.
In 1853 the Irish Industrial Exhibition was
held in Dublin, financed by railway magnate and
entrepreneur William Dargan (*fig. 1*). In addition
to promoting modern design and technological
innovation, the Exhibition also included a Fine
Art Hall (*fig. 2*) where Old Master paintings
attributed to Rembrandt, Poussin, Canaletto
and others evoked an enthusiastic public
response. In recognition of Dargan's exceptional
generosity, a Testimonial Committee was formed
in July 1853 to organise a fitting memorial to
his name. In November of the same year the
Irish Institution was founded to bring into being
a National Gallery and collect works for it.
When these two bodies consolidated their
resources, the results were impressive
and in 1854 an Act of Parliament was passed
establishing the National Gallery of Ireland.

The Irish engineer and architect, Francis Fowke
(1823-1865), who also designed the Royal
Scottish Museum in Edinburgh and what is now
the Cole Wing of the Victoria and Albert Museum
in London, was chosen as architect. The building's
exterior matches the Natural History Museum on
the other side of Leinster Lawn, but has tablets
inscribed with the names of celebrated painters
and sculptors. It was erected at a cost of £28,000
and opened in January 1864 to widespread
popular acclaim. Irish sculptor Thomas Farrell
executed a bronze statue of William Dargan
for the forecourt. Interior features included fire-

3 **Richard Thomas Moynan**
(1856-1906), *Taking
Measurements: the artist copying
the cast of a lion from the
Mausoleum at Halicarnassus
in the National Gallery of
Ireland*, 1887.
Oil on canvas, 99.5 x 62 cm

4 The portico (1903) added
alongside the Dargan (1864)
wing

5 Exterior of the Millennium Wing

proof flooring and top-lit galleries, which were
illuminated by over 2,000 gas burners during the
winter months. A self-portrait of Richard Thomas
Moynan shows him sketching on the ground floor
where there was an extensive display of plaster
casts (*fig. 3*). The original collection comprised
125 paintings with the main room dominated by
17th century Italian canvases. This has grown to
over 2,500 oil paintings and sketches, aside from
almost 9,000 drawings, watercolours, prints,
sculpture and pieces of decorative art. The
building (*fig. 4*) has been extended three times.

The Milltown wing and portico were completed in 1903 (Thomas Newenham Deane), the Beit Wing in 1968 (Frank du Berry) and the Millennium Wing (Gordon Benson and Alan Forsyth), facing onto Clare Street, opened in 2002 with improved public facilities and additional exhibition space (*fig. 5*).

Prior to 1937, when the annual purchase grant was doubled, directors worked with a budget of just £1,000 per annum. Judicious acquisitions during these early years included Rembrandt's LANDSCAPE WITH THE REST ON THE FLIGHT INTO EGYPT (*fig. 6*) in 1883, and Fra Angelico's THE ATTEMPTED MARTYRDOM OF SAINTS COSMAS AND DAMIAN (*fig. 7*) in 1886. There were other notable additions by Mantegna (*fig. 35*), Steen (*fig. 59*), Poussin (*fig. 73*) and Reynolds (*fig. 29*).

Gifts and bequests have played a vital role

6 **Rembrandt** (1606-1669), *Landscape with the Rest on the Flight into Egypt*, 1647. Oil on panel, 34 x 48 cm

7 **Fra Angelico** (c.1395-1455), *Sts. Cosmas and Damian and their brothers surviving the Stake*, c.1440-42. Tempera on panel, 36 x 46 cm

8 **Salomon van Ruysdael**
(c.1600-1670),
The Halt, 1647.
Oil on canvas, 99 x 153 cm

9 **Sarah Cecilia Harrison**
(1863-1941), *Sir Hugh Lane*,
(1875-1915), c.1914.
Oil on canvas, 41 x 31 cm

in enriching the collection. At the beginning of the last century, the Countess of Milltown donated almost two hundred paintings from Russborough House (*fig. 43*). The bequest of ten Dutch and Flemish paintings from Sir Henry Page Turner Barron in 1901 included Salomon van Ruysdael's THE HALT (*fig. 8*) and works by Heda (*fig. 61*) and Brueghel/Rubens (*fig. 53*). Sir Hugh Lane (*fig. 9*) is remembered as one of the most remarkable figures in the history of the Gallery. During his eleven year association, first as a member of the Board from 1904 and later as director 1914-15, he endowed the collection with a series of magnificent gifts. He was tragically killed when the *Lusitania* was torpedoed in 1915. In his will Lane bequeathed purchasing funds which are still active, in addition to a collection of Old Master paintings which included works by Claude Lorrain (*fig. 74*), Snyders (*fig. 54*) and Hogarth (*fig. 26*).

With the Shaw bequest in 1950 the Gallery's finances improved markedly. George Bernard Shaw left one-third of his posthumous royalties to the institution he referred to, in an autobiography,

as 'that cherished asylum of my boyhood'.
A lifesize bronze of him by Troubetzkoy (*fig. 10*),
originally intended for the Embankment in
London, today stands in the Gallery. The Shaw
Fund was the largest source of funds for
acquisitions until comparatively recently and
has also contributed to the Millennium Wing.

A major gift in 1950 came from the Irish-
American mining mogul Sir Alfred Chester Beatty
who presented ninety-three 19th century paintings
to the Nation, including outstanding examples
from the French Realist (*fig. 81*) and Orientalist
traditions. Sir Alfred and Lady Beit's gift in 1987,
of seventeen Dutch, Spanish and British Old
Master paintings, was one of the outstanding
presentations in the history of the collection.
It included works by Vermeer (*fig. 62*), Velázquez
(*fig. 69*) and Gainsborough (*fig. 30*). Amongst

paintings and drawings from the estate of Máire
MacNeill Sweeney, bequeathed the same year,
were seminal canvases by Picasso (*fig. 71*)
and Gris.

The discovery of a long-lost masterpiece
by Caravaggio (*fig. 39*), by the present Keeper
of the collection, in the house of study of the
Jesuit Community on Leeson Street generated
unprecedented public interest. The decision by
the Jesuits (who acknowledge the generosity
of the late Dr Marie Lea-Wilson) to place it on
indefinite loan to the Gallery in 1993 ensured
that it will be appreciated and enjoyed by the
public for generations to come.

In 1997, Sir Denis Mahon, scholar and
collector of 17th century Italian painting,
presented eight works as a future bequest.
These included JACOB BLESSING THE SONS OF
JOSEPH by Guercino and examples by Guido
Reni, Domenichino and Luca Giordano.

Fiscal legislation during the 1990s enabled
the Gallery to acquire two prize works from 18th
century Irish collections, whose locations were
unknown for many years. The scene of music
making by Honthorst (*frontispiece*) was once
owned by the Earl of Charlemont and a statue by
Canova (*fig. 44*), commissioned from the sculptor
by John David La Touche. One can only hope
that the good fortune that has occurred during
the history of the Gallery will continue into
the future.

10 **Prince Paul Troubetzkoy**
(1866-1938), *George
Bernard Shaw, (1856-1950),
Author, Playwright
and Critic*, 1927.
Bronze, 188 cm ht.

Irish Painting

From its origins with portraiture in the mid-17th century and the arrival of landscape painting from the Continent, a strong tradition of painting has developed in Ireland, of which this is the largest public collection.

Throughout the seventeenth and eighteenth centuries, the great majority of Irish painters looked for England for their livelihoods. In 1768 Nathaniel Hone and George Barret were founder members of the Royal Academy in London. Barret trained initially at the Dublin Society Schools before moving to London in 1762 and establishing a successful career as a landscape painter. His VIEW OF POWERSCOURT WATERFALL (*fig. 11*) reveals the influence of Edmund Burke's contemporary essay on the Sublime and the Beautiful. The vastness of this natural phenomenon in Co. Wicklow is emphasised by the small-scale figures in the foreground, who are framed by lofty trees and lit by golden light. Hone's satirical work THE CONJUROR (*fig. 12*)

11 **George Barret**
(1728/32-1784),
*View of Powerscourt
Waterfall*, c.1760.
Oil on canvas,
101.9 x 127.5 cm

12 **Nathaniel Hone**
(1708-1784),
The Conjuror, 1775.
Oil on canvas, 145 x 173 cm

13 **James Barry**
(1741-1806), *Self-Portrait as Timanthes*, face c.1780; completed 1803.
Oil on canvas, 77 x 63.5 cm

14 **Hugh Douglas Hamilton**
(1740-1808), *Frederick Hervey, Bishop of Derry and 4th Earl of Bristol* (1730-1803) *with his grand-daughter Lady Caroline Crichton* (1779-1856), c.1790.
Oil on canvas, 224.4 x 199.5 cm

caused a furore when first exhibited at the Royal Academy in 1775. The subject of an elderly magician conjuring up a painting from a series of Old Master prints was recognised as a direct attack on Sir Joshua Reynolds, President of the Academy, who advocated the study Old Master paintings and had used these sources in his own compositions. The inclusion of a devil to supply the prints and an owl symbolic of folly, underlie the artist's daring parody of an eminent public figure.

The eighteenth century is rich in portraiture. James Barry's SELF-PORTRAIT AS TIMANTHES (*fig. 13*), where he alludes to his personal disappointments, and impressive Grand Tourist portraits by Hugh Douglas Hamilton are distinguished works from the end of the century. Hamilton was the most successful Irish painter to work in Rome. His double portrait of FREDERICK HERVEY, BISHOP OF DERRY AND FOURTH EARL OF BRISTOL, WITH HIS GRAND-DAUGHTER LADY CAROLINE CRICHTON (*fig. 14*) is set against the idyllic lake in the gardens of the Villa Borghese, in Rome. The era witnessed a revival of interest in the ancient art of Greece and Rome. In this painting Lady Caroline draws attention to an antique Roman altar of the twelve gods, then in the Borghese Collection and the type of extraordinary piece that would have appealed to her grandfather.

The impact of the Romantic movement on Irish art is reflected in nineteenth century landscapes by Francis Danby and James Arthur O'Connor. Danby's turbulent THE OPENING OF THE SIXTH SEAL (*fig. 15*) takes its subject from the New Testament Book of Revelation and contrasts the awe-inspiring grandeur of nature with mankind's comparative frailty. In St John's apocalyptic vision, the moon turned red as blood and the stars fell to earth. The painting was so acclaimed that it toured England and America as an individual exhibit.

William Mulready, Frederic William Burton (*fig. 92*) and Daniel Maclise represent the leading Irish artists of the mid-nineteenth century, each establishing successful careers in the fields of genre, watercolour and subject painting. THE MARRIAGE OF STRONGBOW AND AOIFE (*fig. 16*)

15 **Francis Danby** (1793-1861),
*The Opening of the
Sixth Seal*, 1828.
Oil on canvas, 185 x 255 cm

16 **Daniel Maclise** (1806-1870),
*The Marriage of Strongbow
and Aoife*, 1854.
Oil on canvas, 309 x 505 cm

17 **Walter Frederick Osborne**
(1859-1903),
*In a Dublin Park, Light
and Shade*, c.1895.
Oil on canvas, 71 x 91 cm

18 **Roderic O'Conor**
(1860-1940), *Farm at
Lezaven, Finistère*, 1894.
Oil on canvas, 72 x 93 cm

by Maclise is the largest work in the collection.
It illustrates an episode from early Irish history
when the King of Leinster enlisted Norman
support in his battles against the High King.
The wedding of his daughter, Princess Aoife, to
the Norman, Richard de Clare, was a condition
of this military alliance and took place in 1170
following the capture of Waterford. Maclise's
attention to detail and his academic approach
may be seen in his detailed treatment of costumes
and weaponry. The poignant figure of an aged
harpist cradling his broken instrument reflects
the wider damage of a people divided by war.
Patrick MacDowell's A GIRL READING (*fig. 19*)
is very different, being an idealised statue of the
type that established his reputation, with graceful
handling of face and drapery.

From the second half of the 19th to the early
20th centuries, an increasing number of Irish
artists travelled to France, entering Parisian
ateliers and absorbing continental influences
different from the conservative teaching at
home. Nathaniel Hone the Younger inaugurated
this tradition and spent sixteen years with the
Barbizon painters from the early 1850s. He was

followed by others, including Walter Osborne, Roderic O'Conor, Sarah Purser, John Lavery and later William Leech. Brittany was popular with Irish artists during this period. Osborne's charming APPLE GATHERING, QUIMPERLÉ was painted there in 1883. IN A DUBLIN PARK, LIGHT AND SHADE (*fig. 17*) is a later work and illustrates the artist's more Impressionist style just before his untimely death. The dappled sunlight plays upon the seated figures, who can be interpreted as the stages of life from childhood to old age.

O'Conor's vibrant FARM AT LEZAVEN (*fig. 18*) and Leech's tranquil, but equally striking, CONVENT GARDEN, QUIMPERLÉ (*fig. 20*), underscore the significance of Breton subjects for Irish artists. The farm included in O'Conor's painting was a favourite studio on the outskirts of Pont-Aven for *avant-garde* artists. His intense palette of strong colours reveals a debt to the Post-Impressionist artist and friend, Paul Gauguin.

20 **William John Leech** (1881-1968), *Convent Garden, Brittany*, c.1912. Oil on canvas, 132 x 106 cm

19 **Patrick MacDowell** (1799-1870), *A Girl Reading*, 1838. Marble, 141 cm ht.

21 **John Butler Yeats**
(1839-1922), *William Butler*
Yeats (1865-1939),
Author, 1900.
Oil on canvas, 77 x 64 cm

22 **William Orpen** (1878-1931),
The Holy Well, 1916.
Tempera on canvas,
234 x 186 cm

John Butler Yeats (*fig. 21*), William Orpen and John Lavery excelled as gifted portraitists during the early part of the last century. Orpen was also an influential teacher of a new generation of Irish painters, most notably Seán Keating, Margaret Clarke and Patrick Tuohy. His complex satire, THE HOLY WELL (*fig. 22*), with its critique of the West of Ireland as an 'Ideal' Ireland, was painted shortly before he served as a war artist during the First World War and includes portraits of his pupil Keating in full-face and profile.

The establishment of the Society of Dublin Painters in 1920 provided an important outlet for modern art in Dublin. Founder members included Paul Henry, who painted Irish scenes like THE POTATO DIGGERS (*fig. 23*) under the sway of Post-Impressionism, his wife Grace Henry, whose later STILL-LIFE WITH A MARBLE TORSO (*fig. 24*) is an intriguing treatment of a studio interior, Mary Swanzy and Jack B. Yeats. Yeats ranks as one of the finest Irish painters of the 20th century. His *oeuvre* is well represented in the Yeats Museum, with that of his father and sisters. A late expressionistic work, GRIEF (*fig. 25*), evokes the devestation and horror brought by war. Intense pigments, freely applied in bold textural effects, reveal the victims and aggressors in a highly-charged emotive subject. His early style is well shown by the popular LIFFEY SWIM of 1923, which he regarded as a major painting.

23 **Paul Henry** (1876-1958),
The Potato Diggers, 1912.
Oil on canvas, 51 x 46 cm

24 **Grace Henry** (1868-1953),
*Still-life with Marble
Torso,* 1920s.
Oil on canvas, 59.7 x 49.5 cm

25 **Jack B. Yeats** (1871-1957)
Grief, 1951.
Oil on canvas, 102 x 153 cm

British Painting

26 **William Hogarth**
(1697-1764), *The Mackinen Children*, 1747.
Oil on canvas, 180 x 143 cm

The British School spans from the Tudor period to the early 20th century, the strongest section being the 18th century, where artists such as Hogarth, Gainsborough, Reynolds, Romney and Raeburn are well represented.

Portraits are a particular strength and there is often an Irish connection in the sitter or former owner. The collection has grown at a measured pace and there have been notable additions from the Milltown family (Wilson, Reynolds), Lane bequest and Beit Gift (key works by

Gainsborough and Raeburn). Hogarth's WESTERN FAMILY and charming MACKINEN CHILDREN (*fig. 26*) were among fifteen British pictures that had belonged to Hugh Lane. The elder children of William Mackinen, a prosperous sugar plantation owner on Antigua in the West Indies, are shown on a terrace. It is believed that they were painted when in London to complete their education. Elizabeth, aged seventeen, and her brother William, aged fourteen, appear momentarily transfixed by the appearance of a small butterfly which has alighted on a potted sunflower. The butterfly symbolises transient beauty and passing youth adding a touch of melancholy to the scene. The elegant gestures of the young sitters reveal the influence of French Rococo art and though Hogarth is for many synonymous with moral subjects, he was also an admired portraitist and those of children amongst his most delightful creations.

Another noteworthy example of family portraiture from the 18th century is Philip Reinagle's MRS CONGREVE WITH HER CHILDREN (*fig. 27*), the quintessential 'conversation piece', a term used to describe the type of informal group on a small scale fashionable at this period. The painting is one of the best records of how such a room was furnished and laid out. Another interesting feature is that four of the family portraits shown hanging in it are now in the Gallery's possession. These include Kneller's portrait of their ancestor, the dramatist William Congreve, over the fireplace and the central portrait on the back wall, also by Reinagle, depicting the children's father, Captain William Congreve and his eldest son.

Richard Wilson was visiting Italy at the outset of his career when he painted THE TEMPLE OF THE SIBYL, TIVOLI (*fig. 28*), with a pendant view of this popular ancient city near Rome. The celebrated British portrait painter Joshua Reynolds, by whom there are now twelve works in the collection, was also in Rome. His satirical PARODY OF RAPHAEL'S 'SCHOOL OF ATHENS' is filled

27 **Philip Reinagle** (1749-1833),
*Mrs Congreve with her
Children*, 1782.
Oil on canvas, 80.5 x 106 cm

28 **Richard Wilson** (1713-1782),
*The Temple of the Sibyl,
Tivoli*, 1752.
Oil on canvas, 50 x 66 cm

by Grand Tourists, treated with a licence he later
resisted, while his magnificent portrait of CHARLES
COOTE, 1ST EARL OF BELLAMONT (*fig. 29*) presents
a sitter in ceremonial robes. The ornate regalia
includes an exotic ostrich-plumed hat and a
shimmering satin cloak. Even his shoes are
extravagantly decorated with rosettes and metal
spurs. The Earl considered himself a wit and
'man of fashion', but was known as a man whose
'ruling passion was vanity'. The abandonment of
his wife, a daughter of the Duke of Leinster, and
his amorous adventures, earned him a reputation
as 'The Hibernian Seducer'. Reynolds introduces
a further touch of humour into this grandiose
portrayal with a live coote bird perched below the
embroidered one on the banner. This painting is
believed to have hung in the Saloon of Bellamont

Forest, the Earl's County Cavan home. A more restrained, accompanying portrait of the Countess of Bellamont was completed by Reynolds in 1778.

Thomas Gainsborough, contemporary and rival of Reynolds, is represented by ten works. He was one of the most sought after portrait painters of his day, especially by female sitters such as MRS HORTON, but also a fine landscapist. His crisply painted VIEW IN SUFFOLK of about 1746, contrasts markedly with the feathery treatment of landscape in the touching image of THE COTTAGE GIRL (*fig. 30*) with her broken pot, painted near the end of his career.

Francis Wheatley earned a reputation for 'conversation piece' portraits in England before mounting debts and an affair with the wife of a fellow artist, John Gresse, forced him to seek

sanctuary in Ireland between 1779 and 1783. He arrived in November to witness a gathering of the Volunteers to commemorate the birthday of William III. His enormous canvas THE DUBLIN VOLUNTEERS ON COLLEGE GREEN, 4TH NOVEMBER 1779 (*fig. 31*) is a tour de force in the numerous portraits and architectural record of central Dublin, but was not a commercial success. Another example of his fine eye for detail is THE MARQUESS AND MARCHIONESS OF ANTRIM, shown in a carriage against their home at Glenarm, Co. Antrim.

Other distinguished portraits from the British School include LADY ELIZABETH FOSTER (*fig. 32*) shown in a romantic setting as an ancient prophet by Thomas Lawrence and Henry Raeburn's masterpiece SIR JOHN AND LADY CLERK OF PENICUIK (*fig. 33*). Sir John, a wealthy merchant, was the

29 **Joshua Reynolds**
(1723-1792), *Charles Coote,*
1st Earl of Bellamont
(1738-1800), *in robes*
of the Order of the Bath,
1773-74.
Oil on canvas, 245 x 162 cm

30 **Thomas Gainsborough**
(1727-1788),
The Cottage Girl, 1785.
Oil on canvas, 174 x 124.5 cm

31 **Francis Wheatley**
(1747-1801), *The Dublin Volunteers on College Green, 4th November 1779,*
1779-80.
Oil on canvas, 175 x 323 cm

fifth baronet of Penicuik, close to Edinburgh. The tradition of double portraits in Scotland has a lineage to the 17th century and is here perfectly incorporated within a landscape setting. The sitters stand in relatively informal poses against an authentic Scottish moorland backdrop towards which Sir John gestures. The exquisite treatment of light unites figures and landscape, in addition to generating subtle atmospheric effects. He stands against the light, his features partially shadowed. His wife's cheek and dress catch the sunlight which enlivens a distant river in golden highlights.

33 **Henry Raeburn** (1756-1823), *Sir John and Lady Clerk of Penicuik,* 1791.
Oil on canvas, 145 x 206 cm

32 **Thomas Lawrence**
(1769-1830), *Lady Elizabeth Foster* (1759-1824), *later Duchess of Devonshire,* c.1805.
Oil on canvas, 240 x 148 cm

Italian Painting

34 **Paolo Uccello** (1397-1475), *The Virgin and Child*, c.1435-40. Tempera on panel, 58 x 37 cm

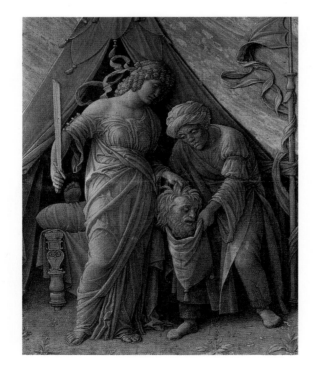

35 **Andrea Mantegna** (1431-1506), *Judith with the Head of Holofernes*, c.1495-1500. Distemper on linen, 48.1 x 36.7 cm

From a core group of 17th century paintings, which has continued to be enhanced, a collection has been built from the Renaissance to the 18th century. There are many artists not easily found outside Italy and have been important additions in recent years.

In 1856, through the agency of Robert MacPherson in Rome, the Governors and Guardians successfully negotiated for thirty-nine paintings. Many of these were formerly in the collection of Cardinal Fesch (1763-1839), Napoleon's uncle. They included two magnificent canvases by Giovanni Lanfranco and the imposing ST CHARLES BORROMEO IN GLORY WITH THE ARCHANGEL MICHAEL by Guilio Cesare Procaccini. At this date Italian paintings comprised more than half the collection and they remain today the second largest School.

Uccello's THE VIRGIN AND THE CHILD (*fig. 34*), purchased in 1909, represents an important early Renaissance work, whose attribution was doubted in the past. It reveals the artist's near obsession with illusionistic effects. Applying a knowledge of mathematical perspective, he has created the illusion of three-dimensional space with the Child appearing to reach playfully beyond the picture plane. The fascination with geometry is particularly evident in the treatment of Christ's face, which has been rendered as a sphere, rather than treated more naturalistically. A less extreme work, with rich colouring, is the Fra Angelico painting (*fig. 7*) with the miraculous survival of Sts. Cosmas and Damian.

Andrea Mantegna's JUDITH WITH THE HEAD OF HOLOFERNES (*fig. 35*), purchased in 1896, is one of the most notable Italian works. Executed towards the end of the 15th century, it illustrates a story from the Old Testament where Judith kills an enemy general. At a time when the Italian peninsula was divided into a series of city states, many small and vulnerable, subjects which

36 **Titian** (c.1480/90-1576),
Ecce Homo, c.1558-60.
Oil on canvas, 73.4 x 56 cm

37 **Giovan Battista Moroni**
(before 1524-1578),
*Portrait of a Gentleman and
his Two Children*, c.1570.
Oil on canvas, 126 x 98 cm

celebrated the triumph of individuals against more
powerful enemies had a particular resonance.
Mantegna enjoyed the patronage of many wealthy
individuals, including Federico Gonzaga, Duke of
Mantua, for whom he worked as court painter
during the latter years of his life. Like many of
his contemporaries, he closely studied and took
inspiration from antique sculpture. This work is
painted in *grisaille*, a technique which employs
neutral tones to imitate the effects of stone.

Titian's tragic ECCE HOMO (*fig. 36*), or Christ as
the mocked king, and Moroni's striking PORTRAIT
OF A GENTLEMAN AND HIS TWO CHILDREN (*fig. 37*),
bought from an unknown London source in
1866, form part of a rich group of 16th century
Northern Italian works. Part of the enigma about
the group portrait is the lack of their mother and
the letter on the table to the left which only
identifies the location as Albino, a small town
close to Bergamo, where the artist was born.
The austere background is a typical device by him
and, coupled with the man's sombre attire, serves
to heighten the intense colours of the children's
garments. Gathering them protectively, he seeks to
shield them from potential harm and an air of
poignancy pervades this intimate family group.

A more festive group of THE VISIT OF THE
QUEEN OF SHEBA TO SOLOMON (*fig. 38*) by Lavinia
Fontana, bought in 1872, contains a series
of female heads clearly based on life and was
executed in Bologna at the height of her career,
conveying the lavish splendour of contemporary

38 **Lavinia Fontana**
(1552-1614), *The Visit of
the Queen of Sheba to
Solomon*, c.1600.
Oil on canvas, 256.5 x 325 cm

39 **Michelangelo Merisi da
Caravaggio** (1571-1610),
The Taking of Christ, 1602.
Oil on canvas, 133.5 x 169.5 cm

40 **Orazio Gentileschi**
(1563-1639), *David and
Goliath*, c.1605-07.
Oil on canvas, 185.5 x 136 cm

court life. She was a rare example of a woman
artist at this date to achieve recognition in her
lifetime and enjoyed a successful career first
in Bologna and later, at the invitation of Pope
Clement VII, in Rome.

The Baroque era is strongly represented with
Caravaggio's outstanding THE TAKING OF CHRIST
(*fig. 39*) certainly the most important work.
It was commissioned from the artist in 1602 by
the Roman nobleman Ciriaco Mattei and depicts
the arrest of Christ following Judas' betrayal.
Christ maintains his composure at a moment
of drama, rendered more emphatic through the
artist's lighting effects. The startling realism of
Caravaggio's figures, tactile quality of armour
and dress, combined with his use of gesture, strike
the viewer on an emotional level. It has been
suggested that the features of the lantern-bearer
are those of Caravaggio himself, who would have
been thirty-one at the time. He painted rapidly,
without the assistance of preparatory drawings,
and changes can be seen both in x-ray and in a
number of alterations or *pentimenti*, now visible
to the naked eye. One of the most obvious is
Judas's ear, originally positioned slightly higher.

One of many artists influenced by Caravaggio
was Orazio Gentileschi, whose DAVID AND GOLIATH
(*fig. 40*), purchased from a London sweetshop in
1937, employs dramatic foreshortening and strong
shadow. Giovanni Lanfranco's MIRACLE OF THE
LOAVES AND FISHES (*fig. 41*), equally full of gesture,
was conceived with THE LAST SUPPER for a chapel
dedicated to the Blessed Sacrament in S. Paolo
fuori le Mura, Rome. Other artists found in the
Baroque Room are Carlo Maratti, Giovanni
Castiglione and the Florentines Cesare Dandini
and Felice Ficherelli.

A number of choice 18th century paintings
includes two views of Dresden by Bernardo
Bellotto (*fig. 42*) in superb condition, which were
acquired in 1883. The Milltown Gift of 1902
brought four Panini landscapes, based on Roman
buildings, and family portraits by Pompeo Batoni.
JOSEPH LEESON, LATER 1ST EARL OF MILLTOWN
(*fig. 43*) sat on the first of two visits to Rome.
This is the artist's earliest identified portrait of
an English-speaking sitter, the start of a vogue
amongst Grand Tourists visiting Italy. Leeson

41 **Giovanni Lanfranco**
(1582-1647),
*The Miracle of the Loaves
and Fishes*, 1624-25.
Oil on canvas,
227 x 423.5 cm

42 **Bernardo Bellotto**
(1721-1780), *Dresden
from the right bank of the
Elbe above the Augustus
Bridge*, c.1750.
Oil on canvas, 51.5 x 84 cm

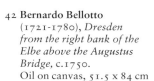

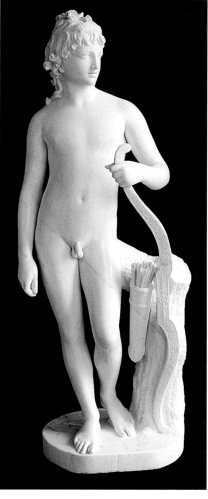

built Russborough House in County Wicklow
to house his painting and sculpture collection
and is shown wearing a fur-lined indoor coat
and fur hat. THOMAS CONOLLY (*back cover*),
who inherited Castletown House, County
Kildare, was painted by Batoni's rival, Anton
Raphaël Mengs. Dressed in a blue coat and
waistcoat trimmed with gold braid, he adopts
a pose like the *Apollo Belvedere* against a
sculpted relief of the Muses. The AMORINO
(*fig. 44*) by Antonio Canova was his third
and most sensitive version of cupid standing
by his bow, with a refined handling
of marble. Acquired in 1998, it is a jewel of
the sculpture collection.

43 **Pompeo Girolamo Batoni**
(1708-1787), *Joseph Leeson*
(1711-1783), *later 1st Earl
of Milltown*, 1744.
Oil on canvas, 137 x 102 cm

44 **Antonio Canova**
(1757-1822),
Amorino, 1789-91.
Marble, 142 cm ht.

German & Early Netherlandish Painting

Though numerically small, there are some choice 16th century German portraits, the period of the largest concentration in the Early Netherlandish School too, where earlier works were only acquired more recently.

Conrad Faber's HEINRICH KNOBLAUCH and his sister KATHERINA KNOBLAUCH (*fig. 45*) are significant portraits by a Frankfurt artist who specialised in this field during the first half of the 16th century, when it was rare for a German artist to do so. Katherina is nineteen years old and set against a panoramic landscape based on the river Danube. Her extensive rings and jewel encrusted garments signify both rank and status. She was a member of the aristocratic

House of Limpburg in Frankfurt like her husband Friedrich Rohrbach, whose pendant portrait is today in the Art Institute of Chicago, having been separated at auction in the 19th century. Since Knoblauch in German means 'garlic', its bulbs are prominently displayed in Katherina's coat-of-arms on the reverse of the panel.

Georg Pencz's PORTRAIT OF A MAN AGED TWENTY-EIGHT indicates the impact of Florentine Mannerist portraiture in the presentation, scale and use of canvas support. The man holds a small bronze of Pan and Luna and is thought to have been a collector. Only his age and the picture's date are inscribed in the background.

Among the infrequent German acquisitions in recent years is Emil Nolde's powerful TWO WOMEN IN A GARDEN (*fig. 47*) purchased with the Shaw

45 **Conrad Faber**
(before 1524-1552),
Katherina Knoblauch
(1512/13-1542), 1532.
Oil on panel, 50.5 x 35.9 cm

46 **Georg Pencz**
(active 1523-1550),
*Portrait of a Man aged
twenty-eight*, 1549.
Oil on canvas, 84.1 x 64.5 cm

47 **Emil Nolde** (1867-1953),
Two Women in a Garden,
1915.
Oil on canvas, 73 x 88 cm

Fund. It reveals the Expressionist artist returning
to the theme of flower painting, composed 'more
profoundly and substantially and filled with more
melancholy', characterised by darker hues and
bold colour contrasts. The freedom with which
pigments have been applied and the use of
expansive brushstrokes reflect the artist's desire
'to bring light and colour into the picture' rather
than simply reproduce nature. Nolde's career was
severely curtailed by the Nazi regime, nethertheless
he produced over a thousand oil paintings and
a large number of works on paper.

The Early Netherlandish School is one of the
smallest in the Gallery and contains several works

48 **Gerard David**
(before 1484-1523),
*Christ bidding Farewell
to His Mother*, c.1510.
Oil on panel, 119.6 x 61.4 cm

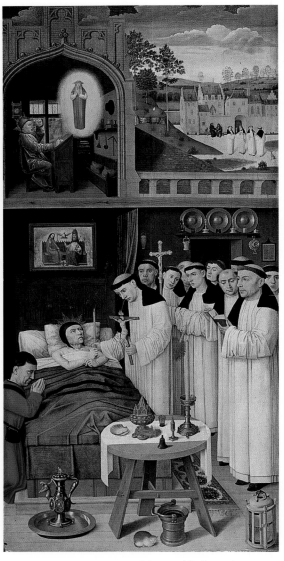

49 **Master of St Augustine**
(active c.1490-1500),
*Scenes from the Life of
St Augustine*, 1490s.
Oil on panel, 136.1 x 66.4 cm

that have been affected by political turmoil and alteration. Gerard David's moving interpretation of CHRIST BIDDING FAREWELL TO HIS MOTHER (*fig. 48*) is inscribed in Latin 'Farewell my sweetest mother I go now to be offered for the salvation of mankind'. By eliminating superfluous detail, employing light to accentuate Christ's features, and the restrained gestures and expression of Christ, David has created an image of compelling psychological depth. It seems likely that he executed a second panel depicting the Virgin,

His Mother, and that they flanked a central one the Virgin and Child.

Dating from a similar period are SCENES FROM THE LIFE OF ST AUGUSTINE (*fig. 49*) by the Master of St Augustine, now separated from a triptych whose central panel is in the Metropolitan Museum of Art, New York. The Master of The Youth of St Romold is a painter identified with scenes of that Saint's life and THE ENTHRONEMENT OF SAINT ROMOLD AS BISHOP OF DUBLIN something of a curiosity in the collection.

It is one of twenty-nine paintings commissioned from various artists between c.1480-1510 for St Romold's Cathedral in Malines and illustrates a key episode from the life of the 8th century Saint, who was killed by dissolute workmen. What is interesting in an Irish context is that St Romold is said to have been consecrated in Dublin, though no historic proof supports this supposition. The artist's delight in richly patterned fabrics is evident, while the somewhat uniform and inexpressive figures typify his hand.

A late example from the Netherlandish School is Pieter Brueghel the Younger's PEASANT WEDDING (*fig. 51*) purchased in 1928. Inspired by the type of scene painted by his father, it is the earliest dated example of many versions and this lively and humorous genre painting rarely fails to captivate viewers. While ostensibly illustrating a wedding, the picture has also been interpreted as representing the seven deadly sins. One detail in the centre of a man reaching up a woman's skirt was revealed again when the painting was cleaned.

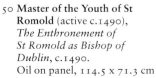

50 **Master of the Youth of St Romold** (active c.1490), *The Enthronement of St Romold as Bishop of Dublin*, c.1490. Oil on panel, 114.5 x 71.3 cm

51 **Pieter Brueghel the Younger** (c.1564-c.1637), *Peasant Wedding*, 1620. Oil on canvas, 81.5 x 105.2 cm

Later Flemish Painting

A substantial number of the Flemish School date from the 17th century and represent the principal types of religious subject, portraiture and landscape.

Jacob Jordaens' overwhelming VENERATION OF THE EUCHARIST was one of only eight Flemish works in the Gallery at the outset and had been acquired for a modest price when such imagery was out of fashion. Jordaens was recognised as the leading painter in Antwerp following the death of Rubens in 1640. This monumental altarpiece, possibly for an Augustinian church, is first recorded in a Dutch sale in 1785. It incorporates a complex religious allegory, whose precise meaning remains elusive.

At the centre, a female figure, seated on a lion, holds forth a monstrance with the Eucharistic wafer. Immediately below, resting on a globe, the Christ Child displays a flaming heart, an emblem of religious fervour. The serpent and human skull at his feet allude to His triumphant victory over sin and death. The four male figures, gathered around him are the Latin Doctors of the Church. Amongst the flanking Saints are Sts. Peter and Paul, with St Sebastian on the right identifiable by his quiver of arrows. An interesting technical detail is the echo of his head to the left. Jordaens evidently altered the position while working on the composition and this change, or *pentimento*, has now become visible.

53 **Jan Brueghel II** (1601-1678) and **Peter Paul Rubens** (1577-1640), *Christ in the House of Martha and Mary*, c.1628.
Oil on panel, 64 x 61.9 cm

52 **Jacob Jordaens** (1593-1678), *The Veneration of the Eucharist*, c.1630.
Oil on canvas, 285 x 235.1 cm

54 **Frans Snyders** (1579-1657),
A Banquet-piece, late 1620s.
Oil on canvas, 92.3 x 158 cm

55 **Anthony van Dyck**
(1599-1641),
*A Boy Standing on
a Terrace*, c.1623-24.
Oil on canvas,
188.3 x 125.3 cm

The intimate scale of the Brueghel/Rubens CHRIST IN THE HOUSE OF MARTHA AND MARY (*fig. 53*) is in marked contrast. It formed part of the Sir Henry Page Turner Barron bequest in 1901 and illustrates an episode from the Gospel of St Luke. Visited by Christ in their home, the two sisters of Lazarus reacted in entirely different ways. Mary sat and listened to His words, while Martha busied herself with household chores. When she grew tired, Martha sought Christ's intervention with her sister, only to be told that Mary 'hath chosen the good part which shall not be taken from her'. The opposition of spiritual and material concerns, or the contemplative and active life, was a popular one in the 17th century and has been translated to the terrace of a large house, where amongst the display of still-life is a symbolic chained tamarin monkey. Within the house a servant is preparing a peacock, a traditional symbol of immortality, whilst also a metaphor for man's pride and love of show. The painting is a collaborative one where figures by Peter Paul Rubens are in a landscape setting by Jan Brueghel II. Long thought to have been cut down to a square shape at a later date, the hitherto missing section on the left has now been acquired. There are also larger altarpieces by Rubens of ST PETER FINDING THE TRIBUTE MONEY and THE ANNUNCIATION.

Amongst the paintings which came from the Lane bequest in 1918 were Frans Snyders' BANQUET-PIECE (*fig. 54*) with an array of objects, fruit and flowers and A BOY STANDING ON A TERRACE (*fig. 55*) by Anthony van Dyck. A former pupil of Rubens, van Dyck established an international reputation as a portraitist and served aristocratic patrons in Flanders, Italy and England. This work comes from the series of portraits carried out for the wealthy families of Genoa in the early 1620s, though the young boy's name is tantalisingly unknown. He poses with the confidence and self-assurance of an adult and the inclusion of a spaniel jumping to lick his hand adds an informal note. Amongst other Flemish pictures is Adam de Coster's A MAN SINGING BY CANDLELIGHT where the influence of Caravaggio is evident.

Dutch Painting

56 **Ferdinand Bol** (1616-1680),
*David's Dying Charge
to Solomon*, 1643.
Oil on canvas, 171 x 230 cm

57 **Jan Steen** (1625/26-1679),
The Village School, c.1665.
Oil on canvas,
110.5 x 80.2 cm

All facets of Dutch 17th century art can be found in the collection – depictions of everyday life, history paintings by Rembrandt and his circle, portraits and landscapes, artists influenced by Italy and exceptional interior subjects by Vermeer and the Delft School.

Artists became increasingly specialised, with still-life and genre (or scenes of everyday life) emerging as independent categories of painting. There was even an annual art fair at Rotterdam by the 1640s where diarist, John Evelyn, was amazed at the quantity for sale and broad social range of purchasers. The earliest Dutch painting to be acquired was the large DAVID'S DYING CHARGE TO SOLOMON (*fig. 56*) by Ferdinand Bol, one of Rembrandt's leading pupils. The scene is of Solomon being named by his father King David as heir, watched by his mother Bathsheba. It was deposited with the Irish Institution in 1854 by the Earl of St Germans, then Lord Lieutenant of Ireland, as a work for the future National Gallery. Though located at his official residence by the early 19th century, the original source remains unknown.

The Dutch School was formed to a great extent by Henry Doyle, director of the Gallery from 1869-92. He purchased almost sixty Dutch paintings, with half his annual funds expended on Rembrandt's LANDSCAPE WITH THE REST ON THE FLIGHT TO EGYPT (*fig. 6*), a gem bought on the spur of the moment at auction. In 1879 he acquired Jan Steen's THE VILLAGE SCHOOL (*fig. 57*), a lively genre scene that remains one of the most popular works in the Gallery. A schoolmaster punishes an inattentive boy with a ferule, or wooden spoon, whilst his classmates react with a mixture of apprehension and humour. A prolific artist, Steen is celebrated for his earthy and humorous subjects, which are underlined by fine draughts-manship and use of colour. Another esteemed Steen painting is THE MARRIAGE SCENE AT CANA from the Beit Gift

58 **Pieter de Hooch** (1629-1684),
Players at Tric-trac, c.1652-55.
Oil on panel, 45 x 33.5 cm

59 **Willem Claesz. Heda** (1593/94-
1680/82), *A Banquet-piece*, c.1635.
Oil on panel, 55.3 x 73.8 cm

in 1987. An early piece by Pieter de Hooch, PLAYERS AT TRIC-TRAC (*fig. 58*), purchased in 1892, with soldiers portrayed as wastrels, is indicative of the many cabinet-size paintings, intended for close study, where the quality of handling often belies the lowly subject matter.

The generosity of benefactors has again been of importance with the Dutch paintings. Sir Henry Page Turner Barron's bequest of 1901 included Salomon van Ruysdael's THE HALT (*fig. 8*) and Willem Claesz. Heda's A BANQUET-PIECE (*fig. 59*). Heda specialised in still-life of domestic objects

60 **Jacob van Ruisdael**
(c.1628/29-1682),
The Castle of Bentheim, 1653.
Oil on canvas, 110.5 x 144 cm

61 **Meindert Hobbema**
(1638-1709), *A Wooded
Landscape: the Path on
the Dyke*, 1663.
Oil on canvas, 105.5 x 128 cm

first Alfred Beit. THE CASTLE OF BENTHEIM (*fig. 60*)
by Jacob van Ruisdael is ranked amongst his
chief works, with its majestic resolution of a
view he painted many times. Likewise, A WOODED
LANDSCAPE – THE PATH ON THE DYKE (*fig. 61*),
by his former pupil Meindert Hobbema, has long
been admired as that artist's most distinguished
work. The 19th century art historian, G.F.
Waagen, described it as 'a picture equal to a whole
gallery'. The subject is a typical Dutch rural scene,
treated with exceptional precision and truth in
the details of trees, fauna and incidents of light.
Hobbema here worked in collaboration with
Adriaen van de Velde who added the figures
and well fed cattle.

Johannes Vermeer's domestic interior LADY
WRITING A LETTER, WITH HER MAID (*fig. 64*) is
one of only thirty-five paintings by the artist in
existence and today one of the most celebrated.
Paintings of letter writing, which often relate to
the theme of love, were much in demand in 17th
century Holland. As a lady concentrates on her
reply, both she and the maid are frozen in the
intense light from a window, while behind them
a painting of 'The Finding of Moses' symbolises

rendered with a craftsmanlike finish and
demonstrating great technical virtuosity. Here
he depicts a cluttered table in the aftermath of a
meal, served with expensive glass and metalware.

The Beit Gift included a group of outstanding
Dutch pictures which had been purchased by the

62 **Gabriel Metsu** (1629-1667),
A Man Writing a Letter,
c.1663.
Oil on panel, 52.5 x 40.2 cm

63 **Gabriel Metsu** (1629-1667),
A Woman Reading a Letter,
c.1663.
Oil on panel, 52.5 x 40.2 cm

the need to trust in Divine Will. Vermeer builds up detail in minute brushwork with layers of colour to produce an unequalled sense of interior light. He produced no more than two or three paintings a year and was to be forgotten after his death for two centuries.

Gabriel Metsu, the contemporary of Vermeer, more overtly explored the theme of love letters with A MAN WRITING A LETTER (*fig. 62*) and A WOMAN READING A LETTER (*fig. 63*). As the woman reads his missive, a maid draws back the curtain protecting a picture from the light, to reveal a seascape. Representations of stormy seas were frequently interpreted at this time as indicating the precarious nature of love. As pendant genre scenes are not often found, it further underscores the preciousness of these two works which show Metsu at the height of his powers in the portrayal of objects and fabrics and the capturing of light.

While the 18th century is represented by only a few paintings, these include the double portrait of JERONIMUS TONNEMAN AND HIS SON JERONIMUS ('THE DILETTANTI') (*fig. 65*) by Cornelis Troost, purchased in 1900, which is recognised as the artist's masterpiece. The ornate interior indicates wealth and privilege. Younger Tonneman wears a suit with gilt brading and plays a flute, an instrument then favoured by the leisured amateur. Troost's painting is highly finished, including tiny details like the powder from the father's wig, which has settled on his more sober outfit. The sculpted relief behind of 'Time revealing truth and banishing slander' would prove ironic when a year later the son was forced to flee Holland after a crime.

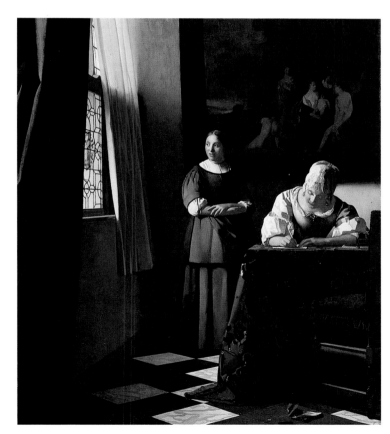

64 **Johannes Vermeer**
(1632-1675), *Lady writing
a Letter, with her Maid*,
c.1670.
Oil on canvas, 71.1 x 60.5 cm

65 **Cornelis Troost** (1696-1750),
*Jeronimus Tonneman
and his son Jeronimus
('The Dilettanti')*, 1736.
Oil on panel, 68 x 58 cm

Spanish Painting

66 **Francisco de Zurbarán**
(1598-1664),
St Rufina, early 1630s.
Oil on canvas, 176 x 107.5 cm

The great period of painting during the 17th century can be well studied in the Gallery alongside examples of early Masters and a number of canvases by Goya.

When the Gallery opened in 1864 there were only four Spanish paintings on view, THE LIBERATION OF ST PETER by José Antolinez having been the first, purchased in 1855. Since then numbers have increased to some fifty-one. Subsequent acquisitions included Murillo's INFANT ST JOHN PLAYING WITH A LAMB in 1869 and Francisco de Zurbarán's IMMACULATE CONCEPTION in 1886. His ST RUFINA (*fig.* 66) was bought in 1933 and is identifiable both by an inscription and the pair of earthenware pots she holds, being the daughter of a potter in Seville who died for her Faith. Zurbarán specialised in such female martyrs and St Rufina hung in the 1830s with sixteen others in the *Galerie Espagnole* of the Louvre.

Thomas MacGreevy, director from 1950-63, purchased a number of high quality Spanish paintings, aided by funds from the Shaw Fund. A great rarity, ABRAHAM AND THE THREE ANGELS (*fig.* 67) by Juan Fernández de Navarrete ('El Mudo') was acquired in 1962. It had been commissioned in 1575 by Philip II of Spain for the monastery palace, El Escorial, where it hung, appropriately, in the Guest Room. The subject relates an Old Testament story of Abraham in old age. He was seated at his doorway when visited by three Angels. Recognising their Divinity, he bathed their feet and provided them with food. They foretold that his wife, Sarah, listening inside, would bear a child, and she laughed in disbelief. The three identical Christ-like figures in the painting also equate them with the three persons of the Holy Trinity. The artist had trained in Venice, from where his treatment of colour and landscape derives and became known as 'The Spanish Titian'.

67 **Juan Fernández de Navarrete**
('El Mudo') (?1538-1579),
Abraham and the Three
Angels, 1576.
Oil on canvas, 286 x 238 cm

In 1962, MacGreevy further acquired THE HOLY FAMILY (*fig. 68*) by Bartolomé Esteban Murillo. This intimate family group, complete with a cat, presents the Virgin and St Joseph as tender parents in a humble domestic setting. The prominence of St Joseph reflects a particular devotion to him in Spain, promoted by St Teresa and the Jesuits. The picture has a interesting

provenance, having been initially brought to London in 1760 when Spanish art was being rediscovered.

In 1987 the Gallery received a number of important endowments. Mrs Alice Murnaghan donated Murillo's monumental MEETING OF JACOB AND RACHEL in memory of her husband. Most importantly, the Beit Gift included eight

paintings, among them Murillo's six scenes illustrating THE PARABLE OF THE PRODIGAL SON. Another highlight was the KITCHEN MAID WITH THE SUPPER AT EMMAUS (*fig. 69*) by Diego Velázquez. Probably the earliest work by him to survive, it shows a half-length figure of a Moorish servant in a kitchen. Through a hatch to the left, Velázquez has added the Supper at Emmaus when Christ revealed himself to incredulous disciples on the day of His Resurrection. The device of combining a kitchen scene with a religious subject was popular in 16th century Flemish painting and here part of a *bodegón*, or subject with genre and still-life, in which Velázquez's skill was acknowledged. Working with a limited palette of ochres, earth tones and white, the modest kitchenware takes on a vivid presence. In less certain times, Francisco de Goya was to record the troubled features of the actress, DOÑA ANTONIA ZÁRATE (*fig. 70*), in a compelling portrait, which completes the Beit Gift.

68 **Bartolomé Esteban Murillo**
(1617-1682),
The Holy Family, 1650s.
Oil on canvas, 205 x 167 cm

69 **Diego Velázquez**
(1599-1660), *Kitchen Maid with the Supper at Emmaus*, c.1617-18.
Oil on canvas, 55 x 118 cm

In the same year, the Máire McNeill Sweeney bequest added two major 20th century Spanish Cubist pictures. Pablo Picasso's STILL-LIFE WITH A MANDOLIN (*fig. 71*) was executed on the Côte d'Azur during the summer of 1924 and contains objects on a table, pared to abstract forms and set above a bright tablecloth with almost dancing pattern. A garden is schematically included behind. The clarity and vibrant colours are evocative of the intense Mediterranean climate. A masked PIERROT by Juan Gris is a theme he explored over a number of years and comments on the role of the artist himself.

70 **Francisco de Goya** (1746-1828), *Doña Antonia Zárate, Actress*, c.1805-06. Oil on canvas, 103.5 x 82 cm

71 **Pablo Picasso** (1881-1973), *Still-life with a mandolin*, 1924. Oil on canvas, 101 x 158 cm

French Painting

72 **Jacques Yverni**
(active 1410-1438),
The Annunciation, c.1435.
Tempera on panel,
151 x 193 cm

73 **Nicolas Poussin** (1594-1665),
*The Lamentation over the
Dead Christ*, 1657/60.
Oil on canvas, 94 x 130 cm

Some of the best-known and attractive
paintings belong to the French School,
of which the majority date from the
17th to 19th centuries, with a number of
internationally recognised masterpieces.

A sole panel from the 15th century, THE
ANNUNCIATION (*fig.* 72) by Jacques Yverni,
shows the impact of the Papal exile in Avignon
on French art and is displayed with the Italian
School. As the Angel Gabriel announces to the
Virgin Mary that she will bear a son, Christ's
Incarnation is shown by the inclusion of a tiny
form conveyed upon divine rays from heaven
towards earth. A slender lily in a pot symbolises
Her purity. The size of the main figures is
according to their holy, rather than earthly, status.
The figure standing to the right is St Stephen, the
first Christian martyr, who was stoned to death
and below him are two smaller kneeling figures,

74 **Claude Lorrain** (1604/5-1682),
*Juno Confiding Io to the care
of Argus*, 1660.
Oil on canvas, 60 x 75 cm

75 **Jean-Baptiste Chardin**
(1699-1779), *Still-life: two
rabbits, a grey partridge,
game bag and powder flask*,
1731.
Oil on canvas, 82.5 x 65 cm

probably the donor and her chaplain, There is
an elegance of line and refinement of detail
in the painting, seen, for example, in the Virgin's
demeanor and arched building in which she
is set.

At the opening of the Gallery, French painting
was barely represented. An early acquisition
was THE LAMENTATION OVER THE DEAD CHRIST
(*fig. 73*)by Nicolas Poussin. He is today regarded
as the finest French history painter of the 17th
century and the Dublin 'Lamentation' considered
by many scholars to be his most distinguished
religious work. It is a deeply moving account of
the moment just prior to Christ being placed in
the tomb when His close followers grieve over
Him. Through colour and the starkness of the
figures our attention is drawn to the figure of the
Virgin in blue, her left hand extended in a gesture
of helpfulness and her right raised to wipe away
her tears.

In the Milltown Gift of 1902 was a further
Poussin of THE HOLY FAMILY, believed acquired by
the 1st Earl of Milltown (*fig. 43*) in Paris and his
most important non-Italian picture. Two further
examples in the Lane bequest of 1918 were ACIS
AND GALATEA and NYMPH AND SATYR DRINKING.
Claude Lorrain's JUNO CONFIDING IO TO THE
CARE OF ARGUS (*fig. 74*) is another Lane picture.
The subject comes from Ovid's *Metamorphoses*,
a popular source of stories, and tells how
Jupiter attempted to deceive his wife Juno by
transforming a river nymph, when he had
seduced, into a beautiful white heifer. Having
obtained her as a gift, Juno entrusted the heifer to
Argus, who according to Ovid was a monstrous
one hundred eyed giant, but who appears here as
a young shepherd. The true glory of the picture is
the idealised landscape and the evocation of dawn
light in the Campagna. From Lane too, came
a STILL-LIFE (*fig. 75*) by Jean-Baptiste Chardin,

where a complex design is combined with subtle colouring, inducing a mood of contemplation rather than triumph after the chase as in two groups of DEAD GAME by Desportes.

Nicolas de Largillière's portrait of the medallist PHILIPPE ROETTIERS (*fig. 76*) was acquired in the 1960s, when use of the Shaw Fund enabled Thomas MacGreevy and James White to fill gaps in the French collection. THE FUNERAL OF PATROCLUS (*fig. 77*) by Jacques-Louis David is an incident about the siege of Troy in Homer's epic *Iliad* and was painted by the artist early in his

career to demonstrate his development while a student in Rome. A fully worked oil sketch, with brilliant colour and high detail, it stands at the end of his rococo period, before the emergence of a more rigorous neo-classical approach. The 18th century study of antiquity is equally found in the ADONIS (*fig. 78*) by François Marie Poncet, which was commissioned in Rome by the Duchess of Leinster's mother and given pride of place in the picture gallery at Leinster House.

Another Shaw Fund picture is the captivating JULIE BONAPARTE, QUEEN OF SPAIN, WITH HER TWO

76 **Nicolas de Largillière** (1656-1746), *Philippe Roettiers*, c.1685. Oil on canvas, 81 x 64 cm

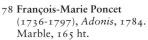

78 **François-Marie Poncet** (1736-1797), *Adonis*, 1784. Marble, 165 ht.

77 **Jacques-Louis David** (1748-1825), *The Funeral of Patroclus*, 1778. Oil on canvas, 94 x 218 cm

79 **François Pascal Simon Gérard**
(1770-1837), *Julie Bonaparte,
Queen of Spain, with her
two Daughters, Zénaïde
and Charlotte*, 1808-09.
Oil on canvas, 200 x 143.5 cm

80 **Jules Breton** (1827-1906),
The Gleaners, 1854.
Oil on canvas, 93 x 138 cm

DAUGHTERS ZÉNAÏDE AND CHARLOTTE (*fig. 79*) by
Baron Gérard. It formed part of a series of five
family groups painted by him for Napoleon's
Salon de Famille at the Palace de Saint-Cloud.
Julie Clary was reputedly of Irish descent and
married Napoleon's younger brother, Joseph,
whom the Emperor briefly placed on the Spanish
throne. Gérard's meticulous technique adds to
the glamour of her satin and velvet dress and
details of hair and furnishings in this magnificent
family record.

The 19th century collection was significantly
enhanced by the Alfred Chester Beatty Gift
in 1950. Amongst Barbizon landscapes and
paintings by Ernest Meissonier and Jacques
Tissot was THE GLEANERS (*fig. 80*) by Jules Breton

acclaimed for its painterly qualities and treatment of what was, at the time, a much debated social issue. LA PEINTURE RÉALISTE (*fig. 81*) by Thomas Couture is a gentle satire on art students who study unadorned nature rather than the Classical past.

The first Impressionist picture acquired was A RIVER SCENE, AUTUMN (*fig. 82*) by Claude Monet, part of a bequest in 1924 from Irish playwright, Edward Martyn, with two pastels by Edgar Degas. Monet explores rapidly changing light and atmospheric conditions, as the trees along the Seine become a blaze of colour. The scene is exhibited alongside works by his contemporaries Alfred Sisley, Eva Gonzalès and Berthe Morisot, which the Shaw Fund enabled to be increased during the 1980s. CHRYSANTHMUMS IN A CHINESE VASE (*fig. 83*) by Camille Pissarro raises a few garden flowers to a timeless image in the tradition of Chardin, yet, at the time, was a diversion when the weather made landscape painting impossible. Paul Signac's LADY ON THE TERRACE (*fig. 84*) brings rigorous colour Divisionism to a peaceful view of St-Tropez in the South of France where the artist's wife stands on the terrace of their villa.

81 **Thomas Couture**
(1815-1879), *La Peinture Réaliste (Realist Painting)*, 1865.
Oil on panel, 56 x 45 cm

82 **Claude Monet** (1840-1926), *A River Scene, Autumn (Argenteuil Basin with a Single Sailboat)*, 1874.
Oil on canvas, 55 x 65 cm

83 **Camille Pissarro**
(1830-1903),
*Chrysanthemums in a
Chinese Vase*, c.1872.
Oil on canvas, 60 x 50.5 cm

84 **Paul Signac** (1863-1935),
Lady on the Terrace, 1898.
Oil on canvas, 73 x 92 cm

Drawings & Watercolours

There is a varied collection of Irish, British and Continental material, whose pattern of collecting has changed markedly since the early years.

Captain Archibald Taylor's 1855 bequest of eighty watercolours (*fig. 2*) were on display from the opening of the Gallery in an upper room. Acquisitions in the Old Master field began auspiciously at the 1866 Henry Wellesley sale, with Italian Renaissance sheets, such as Andrea Mantegna's portrait of the inscrutable FRANCESCO GONZAGA, 4TH MARCHESE OF MANTUA (*fig. 88*), one of very few drawings by him. From the James sale in 1891 came Jean-Antoine Watteau's exquisite WOMAN SEEN FROM THE BACK (*fig. 89*) with three other studies. The opening of the National Portrait and Historical Gallery in 1884 marked

a shift to portraiture and topography. THE CUSTOM HOUSE, DUBLIN (*fig. 90*) by James Malton is one of twelve watercolours in the collection from his famous record of Dublin buildings and street life around 1790. Both Henry Doyle and his successor Walter Armstrong acquired Dutch 17th century drawings in tandem with Dutch paintings, while, in 1900, Henry Vaughan bequeathed thirty-one J.M.W. Turner watercolours. These brilliant landscapes, like THE DOGE'S PALACE AND PIAZZETTA (*fig.91*) from Turner's last visit to Venice, continue to attract considerable attention when they are exhibited annually during January. Another bequest the same year, from Margaret Stokes, of George Petrie and Frederic William Burton studies, included Burton's MEETING ON THE TURRET STAIRS (*fig.92*). Inspired by a tragic love story in Norse saga, this is today one of the most

88 Attributed to **Andrea Mantegna** (1431-1506), *Francesco Gonzaga, 4th Marchese of Mantua* (1466-1519), c.1495. Black chalk with wash and white highlights on paper, 34.8 x 23.8 cm

89 **Antoine Watteau** (1684-1721), *Woman seen from the back*, c.1715. Red chalk and pencil on paper, 14 x 9.5 cm

90 **James Malton** (c.1760-1803),
*The Custom House,
Dublin*, 1793.
Watercolour over ink on
paper, 53.6 x 77 cm

91 **Joseph Mallord William
Turner** (1775-1851),
*The Doge's Palace and
Piazzetta, Venice*, 1840.
Watercolour and red ink
on paper, 24 x 30.4 cm

requested watercolours. The purchase in 1901
of forty Burton drawings and watercolours was
the start of acquiring extensive studio contents.
There are also the original drawings used in the
Dublin Society Drawing Schools and a group
of European miniatures (transferred from the
National Museum of Ireland in 1966 and 1969).
In addition there have been numerous individual
purchases and gifts. The Print Gallery holds
internal and loan exhibitions and other works
on paper can be inspected by appointment in
the Print Room, or, in the Yeats Archive.

92 **Frederic William Burton**
(1816-1900), *The Meeting
on the Turret Stairs*, 1864.
Watercolour on paper,
95.5 x 60.8 cm

Greek and Russian Painting (Icons)

In 1968, Director James White purchased twenty-four icons from the collection of W.E.D. Allen, a much travelled scholar and former military attaché. Ikon in the Greek language means 'image' and the term was used to describe representations of Christ, the Virgin, and Saints, which were painted on wood, as opposed to wall paintings. They were used as objects of veneration in the Greek Orthodox world from about the 6th century. Byzantine, Greek and Russian icons are all represented in the Gallery, with the earliest examples dating to the 14th century.

Icons were traditionally painted in a tempera medium on well-seasoned wood: lime, birch and oak being popular supports. They were generally displayed in carefully ordered tiers on the Iconostasis, the screen which divided the sanctuary from the nave in an Orthodox church. The creators of these restrained and deeply spiritual images adhered to prescribed conventions both in terms of style and subject matter. THE VIRGIN AND CHILD HODIGITRIA, WITH JOHN THE BAPTIST AND TWELVE PROPHETS (*fig. 85*), by an artist of the Constantinople School, represents the

Virgin in her role as 'Indicator of the Way'. Frontally posed and dressed in Imperial purple, she gestures towards her Son as Saviour of the world. The half-length figures of prophets included on the border were a later addition. They hold scrolls which refer to the coming of Christ as well as their appropriate emblems.

Amongst the finest icons is an early 15th century Russian depiction of ST GEORGE AND THE DRAGON (*fig. 86*) from the Novgorod School. At this time St George was widely venerated in the districts of northern Russia; his slaying of the dragon implying the victory of Christianity over paganism. In this dream-like image, the Saint is blessed from above by the Saviour's hand and attended by St Nicholas. A rhythmic linear treatment distinguishes the work and the vibrant red is a typical pigment used by Novgorod artists. The elongated figures and muted colouring of THE ENTRY INTO JERUSALEM (*fig. 87*) meanwhile demonstrates the influence of the Greek, Dionysius, on late 15th century Moscow School painters.

85 **Constantinople School** (c.1325; Margin 15th century), *The Virgin and Child Hodigitria, with John the Baptist and Twelve Prophets.* Tempera on panel 135 x 111 cm

86 **Novgorod School** (early 15th century), *The Miracle of St George and the Dragon.* Tempera on panel, 73.5 x 63 cm

87 **Moscow School** (late 15th century), *The Entry into Jerusalem* Tempera on panel, 33.5 x 26 cm

Support for the Gallery

Development Office

The National Gallery of Ireland is a registered charity and donations are always welcome. The Gallery acknowledges the generous support of the many companies who also assist its varied programmes, such as exhibitions, events, research and publications. Corporate involvement with exhibitions in the Millennium Wing offers significant opportunities for companies. It is also an excellent environment for corporate entertainment.

The British Fund for the National Gallery of Ireland has been established in Britain as a charity to raise visibility and contributions towards development and education work. Contributions are potentially tax deductible as allowed by the UK Inland Revenue.

For further information please contact the Development Office. The National Gallery of Ireland, Merrion Square West, Dublin 2. Tel: (353-1) 663 3512. Fax: (353-1) 676 1620. email: orla.obrien@ngi.ie

The National Gallery of Ireland Shop

The Gallery Shop stocks one of the largest selections of books on painting, decorative arts, sculpture, architecture and design in the country, together with numerous catalogues of the Gallery's collections. There is a special section for children's art books. In addition to cards there are prints from the Gallery's collection and an extensive array of beautiful gifts. Income from the shop is a major support for the Gallery. Tel: (353-1) 678 5450. Fax: (353-1) 661 9898. *You can now shop on-line as well at* eshop@nationalgallery.ie

88-90, Merrion Square. Nos. 88-89 today contain the Gallery's administration while No. 90 has been restored as a townhouse and is the headquarters of the Friends.

The Friends of the Gallery

Individual membership. With the establishment of The Friends of the National Gallery of Ireland in 1990, the National Gallery entered a closer relationship with its public. As a support group, it is intended to stimulate an interest in all aspects of art through a busy programme of activities, which focuses not only on the Gallery's own collections, but also on art and architecture across Ireland and abroad.

Patrons of Irish Art. This smaller group within the Friends organisation exists to assist with the acquisition of Irish works of art for the collection. They have acquired paintings by James Latham and Francis Bindon and contributed to works by George Mullins, Hugh Douglas Hamilton, Frederic Burton and Jack B. Yeats. Patrons may participate fully in all events organised by the Friends, as well as enjoying special events organised to acknowledge their support.

Corporate membership. By associating with the Gallery, corporations share in the recognition and prestige which attaches to the operation of the nation's most popular cultural institution. Their support informs the public of a company or organisation's commitment to Irish society, its culture and the education of further generations. Corporate members enjoy all the benefits of regular membership, together with reduced charges for the use of rooms in No. 90.

Annual Subscription. Individual €50. Concession €35. Family €65. Patrons of Irish Art €450. Corporate €650.

Tel: (353-1) 661 9877. email: friendng@gofree.indigo.ie

Gallery Plan

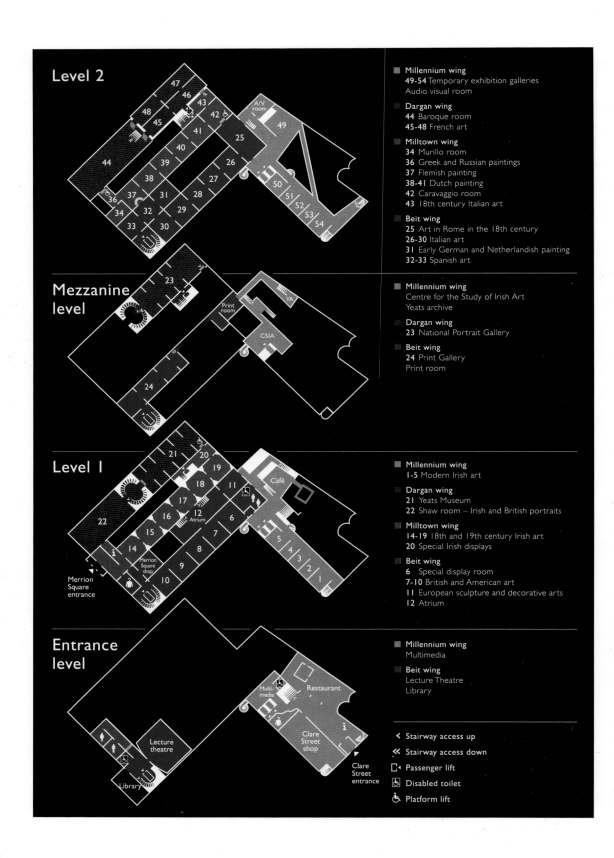

Level 2

47
46
43
48 A/V room
45
42
41 49
40
25
44 39
26
38
37 31 28 27
36 34 32 29 50
33 30 51 52 53 54

■ **Millennium wing**
49-54 Temporary exhibition galleries
Audio visual room

■ **Dargan wing**
44 Baroque room
45-48 French art

■ **Milltown wing**
34 Murillo room
36 Greek and Russian paintings
37 Flemish painting
38-41 Dutch painting
42 Caravaggio room
43 18th century Italian art

■ **Beit wing**
25 Art in Rome in the 18th century
26-30 Italian art
31 Early German and Netherlandish painting
32-33 Spanish art

Mezzanine level

23
Print room
CSIA
24

■ **Millennium wing**
Centre for the Study of Irish Art
Yeats archive

■ **Dargan wing**
23 National Portrait Gallery

■ **Beit wing**
24 Print Gallery
Print room

Level 1

21 20
19
18 11 Café
17 12 Atrium
22 16 6
15 5
14 4 3 2 1
Merrion Square shop
Merrion Square entrance
10

■ **Millennium wing**
1-5 Modern Irish art

■ **Dargan wing**
21 Yeats Museum
22 Shaw room – Irish and British portraits

■ **Milltown wing**
14-19 18th and 19th century Irish art
20 Special Irish displays

■ **Beit wing**
6 Special display room
7-10 British and American art
11 European sculpture and decorative arts
12 Atrium

Entrance level

Multi-media Restaurant
Clare Street shop
Lecture theatre
Library
Clare Street entrance

■ **Millennium wing**
Multimedia

■ **Beit wing**
Lecture Theatre
Library

< Stairway access up
« Stairway access down
⌐◄ Passenger lift
♿ Disabled toilet
♿ Platform lift